A First Book of Prayers

Written and compiled by

Glenda Trist

Illustrated by

Julie Downing and Nadine Wickenden

To my children
Luke, Sophie,
Lily, and Grace,
whose prayers of faith
and expectation have fed
me and encouraged my
own journey of faith.

A First Book of Prayers

Written and compiled by
Glenda Trist

Illustrated by
Julie Downing and
Nadine Wickenden

Senior editor Marie Greenwood
Assistant editor Kritika Gupta
US editor Rebecca Warren
Senior art editor Katie Knutton
Art editor Roohi Rais
Jacket designer Amy Keast
Jacket co-ordinator Francesca Young
Managing editor Laura Gilbert
Managing art editors Neha Ahuja Chowdhry, Diane Peyton Jones
DTP designer Sachin Gupta
Producer, pre-production Nikoleta Parasaki
Producer Srijana Gurung

ORIGINAL EDITION
Commissioning editor Elrose Hunter
Project editor Shaila Awan
Senior art editor Diane Thistlethwaite
Senior editor Linda Esposito
Production Josie Alabaster
Picture research Anna Grapes
Jacket design Simon Oon

First American Edition, 2017
Published in the United States by DK Publishing
345 Hudson Street, New York, New York 10014

Copyright © 2017 Dorling Kindersley Limited
DK, a Division of Penguin Random House LLC
17 18 19 20 21 10 9 8 7 6 5 4 3 2 1
001–298701–Feb/2017

A catalog record for this book is available from the Library of Congress.

ISBN 978-1-4654-6333-3

DK books are available at special discounts when purchased in bulk
for sales promotions, premiums, fund-raising, or educational use.
For details, contact: DK Publishing Special Markets,
345 Hudson Street, New York, New York 10014
SpecialSales@dk.com

Printed and bound in China

A WORLD OF IDEAS:
SEE ALL THERE IS TO KNOW
www.dk.com

Contents

"Prayer is conversation with God"

CLEMENT OF ALEXANDRIA

---

*Prayer is, quite simply, the way our hearts turn
toward God to listen and respond to him.
As adults, we may need to regain
a childlike approach to prayer, but children are
naturally spontaneous and tend easily toward trust
and faith. There is much we can learn from
a young child about prayer!*

Prayer in daily life

Recognizing that children are naturally open to prayer, what can we do to encourage and develop their lifelong pursuit of it? We can create an environment for our children where prayer becomes a natural, daily part of life. Prayer can be presented as an enjoyable conversation with someone we love and trust. Prayers of praise and thanksgiving are preferable, since these come naturally and easily to children. We can help our children turn happy events and small joys into prayers. Simple needs or concerns that arise in our children can also be turned into prayers: sick pets, lost toys, skinned knees. Your child's own walk of faith has begun, and yours is strengthened as you experience prayer together.

Teaching a child to pray

This book is a collection of short, simple prayers designed to help your child develop an awareness of God. Share these simple prayers with your child, and enjoy a special time of love together.

The prayer that Jesus taught us

Our Father in heaven,
hallowed be your name,
your kingdom come,
your will be done on earth as in heaven.
Give us today our daily bread.
Forgive us our sins
as we forgive those who sin against us.
Lead us not into temptation,
but deliver us from evil.
For the kingdom, the power,
and the glory are yours, now and for ever.

Amen.

Prayers about my feelings

Sometimes we feel happy
because we had a good time.
Then it's good to say
thank you to God.
At other times we may feel
lonely, angry, or sorry.
God wants us to tell him
about those feelings, too.

I smile when I am happy

I smile when I am happy.
I scream when I am scared.
I frown when I am jealous.
I cry when I am sad.
Thank you, God, for all
these feelings, good or bad.

Amen.
Lily

I will praise you, O Lord

I will praise you, O Lord,
with all my heart;
I will tell of all your wonders.
I will be glad and rejoice in you;
I will sing praise to your name,
O Most High.

Amen.
PSALM 9:1–2 NIV

You made the thunder

Dear God,

You made the thunder.
It's just like when I'm angry.
You made things just like our feelings.
So you know how I feel.
Help me not to be angry.

Amen.
Grace

It's not fair!

Dear God,

It's not fair!
And I'm really, really mad.
And I hate my mom and my sister!
And I wish they'd go away.
I don't really.
But I needed to say that to someone.
Thanks for listening, God.

Amen.

Please help me not to feel mad

Dear Jesus,

Please help me not to feel mad because it makes me feel bad.

Amen.

When I am quiet

Dear God,

When I am q
I sit by my
and thin
you are
And t

Ame
Gra

I want someone to play with

Dear Jesus,

I want someone to play with.
But everyone else already
has someone to play with.
_t me.
_and lonely.
_member just how
_e, Jesus.
_e feel better,

_friend.

quiet
self
k about how
all around me.
at makes me feel happy.
n.
ce

15

Excep
I feel sad
Help me to re
much you love me
Because that makes n
like I'm not all alone.
Because I know you are my

Amen.

We had the giggles today!

Dear God,

We had the giggles today!
There were so many funny things
to laugh at with each other.
And we were doing
lots of silly things,
Such as funny faces, silly rhymes,
And jumping on the beds.
Thank you for a fun time!
Love from me.

Amen.

I don't think
anybody loves me today

Dear Jesus,

I don't think anybody loves me today.
Everybody's grumpy and mad.
But you're not.
You love me like I'm special. Always.
I'm glad I'm your friend today.

Amen.

Praise to the God and Father

Praise to the God and Father
of our Lord Jesus Christ,
the Father of compassion
and the God of all comfort,
who comforts us in all our troubles.

Amen.
2 CORINTHIANS 1:3 NIV

Prayers about animals

Animals are a wonderful part of God's creation. They are there for us to enjoy, but God also wants us to look after the animals and protect them.

You made some pretty strange animals

Dear God,

You made some pretty strange animals.
A kangaroo with huge feet
and a pocket for its baby,
spiders with no neck and
eight legs to trip over,
and fruit bats that can only sleep
upside down hanging on a tree!
I think you are very clever,
but I think you
must also love to laugh!
Me too.

Amen.

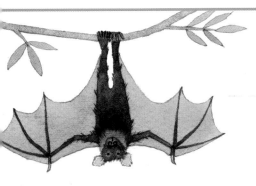

Thank you for making animals

Dear God,
Thank you for making animals
so that we can enjoy them as pets,
or see them in the zoo and in the wild.
Please help people to stop
harming animals.

Amen.
Lindsay

Lord, you have made so many things!

Lord, you have made
so many things!
How wisely you made them all!
The earth is filled with
your creatures…
large and small alike.
All of them depend on you
to give them food when they need it.
You provide food and they
are satisfied.

Amen.
PSALM 104:24–28 GNB

Today I played with my dog

Dear God,

Today I played with my dog.
I had a ball and threw it.
And my dog brought it back
for me to throw again every time.
And it was really slobbery!
I just wanted to thank you for my dog.
We're good friends.

Amen.

Hear and bless your beasts

Dear Father,

Hear and bless
your beasts and singing birds,
and guard with tenderness
small things that have no words.

Amen.
ANON

Thank you for our hamster

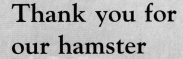

Dear Lord,

Thank you for our hamster.
Thank you that we can cuddle and pet her.
Thank you that she is cute and furry
and nice to look at.
Please help us to take care
of her properly.

Amen.
Timmy

25

Prayers about my day

God makes each day brand-new for us. It is great to know that God goes with us through each day and wants us to talk to him about the things we do and the people we share our day with. These things are important to him, too.

Today is a new day

Dear Jesus,

Today is a new day
and I am one day older.
I can do lots for you today!
Help me to be kind and helpful.
Help me to wait my turn and
tidy up my things.
Help me to have fun and enjoy
your wonderful world!

Amen.

Thank you for helping me

Dear Jesus,

Thank you for helping me
with my spelling test at school.
I want you to help me always.
With love,
Jonathan

Amen.

Thank you for my school

Dear God,

Thank you for my school.
My teachers are nice and
I enjoy school most days.

Amen.

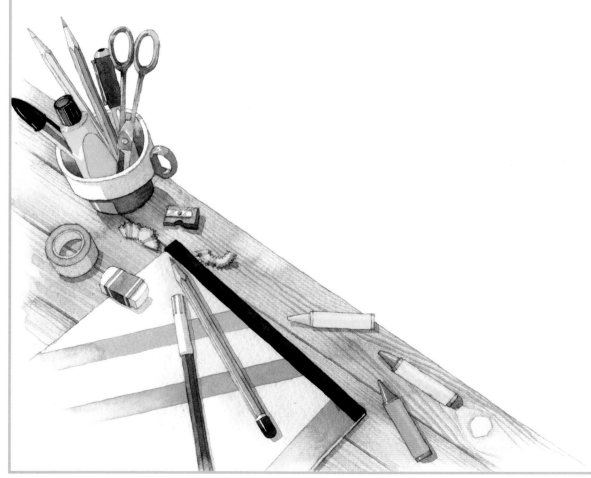

God be in my head

God be in my head and in my understanding;
God be in my eye and in my looking;
God be in my mouth and my speaking;
God be in my heart and in my thinking.

Amen.
MARIA WARE

I am learning to read

Dear Jesus,

I am learning to read
and that makes me feel smart.
Thank you for giving me a good brain
and making me smart.
I'm going to like reading.

Amen.

Thank you for this lovely meal

Dear God,

Thank you for this lovely meal,
and also for the people who made it.
Please help those who don't have food.
In Jesus' name,

Amen.
Lily

I went on the train today

Dear God,

I went on the train today,
and out of the window I could see
all the trees and houses whizzing by.
When you're up in heaven, God,
do you see everything on earth whizzing by
as the world spins around?

Amen.

Thanks for today

Dear God,

Thanks for today,
for being with friends
and for dressing up and
doing concerts and
having fun.

Amen.

Thank you for the day today

Dear God,

Thank you for the day today,
and for my family.
I liked it when we saw all the ants
marching in a line.

Amen.
Larissa

Thank you for the world so sweet

Thank you for the world so sweet.
Thank you for the food we eat.
Thank you for the birds that sing.
Thank you, God, for everything.

Amen.
E. Rutter Leatham

It's time for me to go to bed

Dear Jesus,

It's time for me to go to bed.
But I don't feel safe in the dark.
My mind tells me there are things in the dark—
scary, moving things that I don't like.
Please stay awake when I fall asleep
and protect me from anything that might
hurt me or make me afraid.
Thank you for keeping me safe last night.
Please do the same tonight.

Amen.

Thank you for shiny stars

Dear Jesus,

Thank you for shiny stars at night,
for bedtime stories,
and goodnight cuddles.
Thank you for my warm bed
and quilt to hide under.
Thank you that I feel safe
and cozy and sleepy.
Goodnight, Jesus.

Amen.

When I lie down

When I lie down,
I go to sleep in peace;
you alone, O Lord,
keep me perfectly safe.

Psalm 4:8 GNB

Prayers about my friends

*Friends are precious
and we want to tell
Jesus about them.
Jesus is our best friend.
From him we can learn
how to be a good friend
to others.*

Thank you for my friends

Dear Jesus,

Thank you for my friends.
We have such a good time together.
Every day I can't wait to see them!

Amen.

Breathe on me, breath of God

Breathe on me, breath of God:
fill me with life anew,
that as you love, so I may love
and do what you would do.

Amen.
E. Hatch

It's great to be your friend

Dear Jesus,

It's great to be your friend.
I like having you with me every day.
I like talking with you at any time.

Amen.

Jesus, friend of little children

Jesus, friend of little children,
be a friend to me.
Take my hand and ever keep me
close to thee.

Amen.
WALTER JOHN MATTHEWS

I was awful today

Dear God,

I was awful today and called
someone stupid names.
I didn't stop to think how
it would make them feel.
I'm sorry, God.
Please help me to stop
being mean and to think
about others.

Amen.

I need a friend

Please Jesus,

I need a friend.
I would be kind and share
and play what she wanted
to play most of the time!
Please send me a friend.

Amen.

My friend is sick

Dear God,

My friend is sick,
and I don't want him to be sick.
And I know he doesn't want to be sick.
We want to play together.
Please, please, make him better.

Amen.

Thank you, God, for sleepovers

Thank you, God,
for sleepovers with a friend.
It's more fun, playing with a friend.
Thank you, God,
for being able to rollerblade with a friend.
I would be lonely without my friends.

Amen.
Alison

Thank you for our friends and family

Thank you for our friends and family.
If we did not have any friends,
we would be sad and lonely.
Help people not to judge other
people by their skin or religion.

Amen.
Lacey

Prayers about my family

*God gives us family to love
and care for us.
We can talk to him about
the tough times
and the great times
in our family.*

Most gracious Father

Most gracious Father,
visit this family and household
with thy protection.
Let thy blessing descend and rest
on all who belong to it.

Amen.
JOHN CHARLES RYLE

My mom loves me

Dear Jesus,

My mom loves me. My dad loves me.
And my grandma and my grandad love me, too.
My whole family loves me!
Thank you for my family, Jesus.
Thank you that you gave us families
to teach us how you care for us.

Amen.

Was your mom lovely?

Dear Jesus,

Was your mom lovely?
Did she smell nice
and did she take good care of you?
My mom does.
And she gives wonderful cuddles
and knows special secrets for us to share.
Thank you for giving us moms!

Amen.

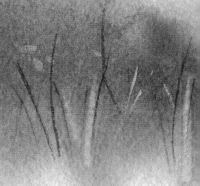

You gave me a great dad

Father God,

You gave me a great dad
here on earth as well.
He plays games with me and
can carry me on his shoulders.
I hope to be like him one day.
Thank you for my dad.
With love,

Amen.

Please bless Mom

Dear God,

Please bless Mom.
Please bless Dad.
Please bless my brother and sister
and help us not to fight.
Please bless Grandma and Grandad
and make them come to visit.
And God bless me and help
me to grow tall fast!

Amen.

I want to thank you

Dear God,

I want to thank you for a very special gift
you have given our family.
My mom has a new baby!
He's really cute and has tiny fingers and toes!
(And now I'm not the baby in the family!)

Amen.

No wonder we are happy in the Lord

No wonder we are happy in the Lord!
For we are trusting him.
We trust his holy name.
Yes, Lord, let your constant love surround us.

PSALM 33:21–22 SLB

Please help my mom and dad

Dear God,

Please help my mom and dad
get all their jobs done
so they can play with me.

Amen.

Today my mom
and dad had a fight

Dear God,

Today my mom and dad had a fight.
They sounded like they really hated each other.
It made me scared.
God, you know I love them both.
Please take care of them and teach them to love
all the good things about each other.

Amen.

It's not fair, God

It's not fair, God,
you were meant to make
this world a good place!
So why are there brothers?
Stupid idiot brothers.
You just can't expect me to love him!
But I know you do.
Dear God, I'm glad
you are so strong because
I need a lot of help from you
to love someone
I'm very angry with!

Amen.

Our family is really small

Dear God,

Our family is really small.
Just me and my mom.
My mom looks after me
and goes to work.
She does everything.
I love my mom.
Please look after her every day.

Amen.

Bless Grandad and Grandma

Please Lord,

Bless Grandad today and help him to
feel better tomorrow.
Please bless all our family today and
please help Grandma
while she's looking after Grandad.

Amen.
Larissa

Prayers about special days

There are some days that are full of good memories— parties, celebrations, special places to go, favorite people to be with.

I love Christmas Day

Dear God,

I love Christmas Day.
It is fun when we open our presents.
Christmas is really about Jesus being born.

Amen.
Ian and Jasmine

This is the day

This is the day which the Lord hath made:
let us rejoice and be glad in it.
For the beloved and most holy child had been
given to us and born for us by the wayside
and hid in a manger because he had
no room in the inn.
Glory to God in the highest
and on earth peace to men of good will.

Amen.
FROM ST. FRANCIS' VESPERS
FOR CHRISTMAS

With shepherds we watch

Dear God,

With shepherds we watch;
with kings we adore;
with angels we sing.
Praise your son evermore.

Amen.

Easter is really hard to understand

Dear Jesus,

Easter is really hard to understand.
Why was Good Friday good if you died?
Why did you have to die?
Please help me to understand.
I'm glad you came alive again, though.
That I can be happy about!

Amen.

Forgive me, please

Dear Jesus,

Forgive me, please,
for all the wrong or selfish things that I do.
Come into my life and make me brand-new
with the life you had when you came alive
again on Easter Day.

Amen.

Thank you for birthdays

O Lord,

Thank you for birthdays.
Thank you for all the excitement
and fun on birthdays—for parties
and presents and the friends
who bring us presents.
We pray for those who can't have parties
or presents on their birthdays.
We pray that they will still be able to
celebrate their special day.

Amen.
Timmy

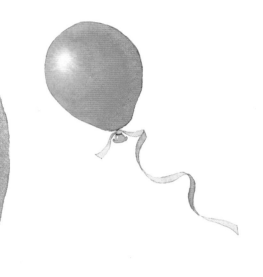

I'm so excited

Dear Jesus,

I'm so excited
I'm going to have a birthday party
with a special cake
and games and balloons.
Thank you, Jesus, thank you!
Please help my friends
to have fun, too!

Amen.

Thank you for my birthday

Dear God,

Thank you for my birthday.
Thank you for my friends and family,
who make me feel special.
Help me to grow more like you
between now and my next birthday.

Amen.

We are moving today

Dear God,

We are moving today.
I'm going to miss all my friends very, very much.
I hope that I will find new friends at my new house.
I will miss my bedroom, too.
But my new house is good
for playing hide-and-seek in,
and that will be exciting.

Amen.
Sophie

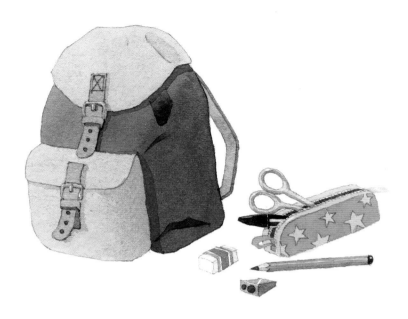

I'm starting school!

Dear Jesus,

Guess what's happening tomorrow!
I'm starting school!
It's so exciting. I'm a big kid now.
But what if I get lost?
I hope I find a friend.
Please be with me
at school today, Jesus.

Amen.
Sophie

I love the sea, Jesus

I love the sea, Jesus.
I love the waves that chase me on the wet sand.
I love the shells and making seaweed drawings.
I love the sand and digging holes and burying my legs.
Jesus, I love you even more for making the sea.

Amen.

I think every day is special

Dear Jesus,

I think every day is special
because you made it!

Amen.

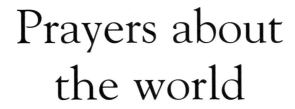

Prayers about the world

*Our world is a big place.
There is so much to see and
do. We can tell God about our
delight in our world and
our worries about it.
We know he cares
about the world.*

Thanks for the great day

Thanks for the great day we had today;
For the sun and playing outside.
I enjoyed the grass and the trees
and those flowers we saw.
I enjoyed lots of things about
the world today, God,
Beautiful things that you made.
Thanks for thinking of us
when you made the world.
Thanks for making things
that we can enjoy each day.

Amen.

We shall have this day only once

Dear Lord Jesus,

We shall have this day only once.
Before it is gone, help us to do all the good we can,
so that today is not a wasted day.

Amen.
STEPHEN GRELLET

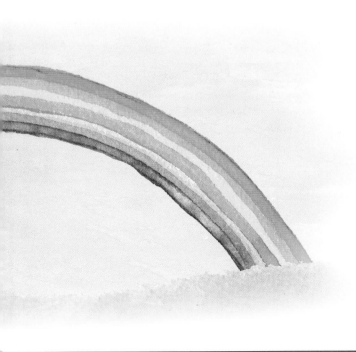

Help the people who
live on the street

Please God,

Help the people who live on the street
to get a home to live in.
And help them to get clothes to wear and food to eat.

Amen.
Amy

Help us to be honest
with each other

Dear God,

Help us to be honest with each other and to
talk with each other whatever color or religion we are.
Help us to make peace around the world
so it can become a friendly place.
Help us to share our things and not to be greedy.

Amen.
Sophie

Please stop the wars and fighting

Dear Jesus,

Please stop the wars and fighting.
People are getting hurt.
Children too.
Please give food to the many hungry families
who have no food for tomorrow.
I know you care about these people, too.

Amen.

You created the day and the night

You created the day and the
night, O God.
You set the sun and the moon
in their places;
you set the limits of the earth;
you made summer and winter.

Amen.
PSALM 74:16–17 GNB

Thank you for the wonderful world

Dear Father,

Thank you for the wonderful world
that you created for us to live in.
Please help us to look after the world
and all the creatures in it.

Amen.
Susanna

Index of prayers

Acknowledgments

Scripture quotations [marked NIV] taken from the *Holy Bible*, New International Version Anglicised Copyright © 1979, 1984, 2011 Biblica. Used by permission of Hodder & Stoughton Ltd, an Hachette UK company. All rights reserved. "NIV" is a registered trademark of Biblica UK trademark number 1448790.

Scripture quotations marked (TLB) are taken from *The Living Bible* copyright © 1971. Used by permission of Tyndale House Publishers, Inc., Carol Stream, Illinois 60188. All rights reserved.

Bible quotations taken from the *Good News Bible* (GNB) reprinted by permission of Harper Collins Publishers Ltd © 1992.

Chapter opener background: 123RF: Liliia Rudchenko/ rudchenko

Please help me not to feel mad

Dear Jesus,

Please help me not to feel mad
because it makes me feel bad.

Amen.

When I am quiet

Dear God,

When I am quiet
I sit by myself
and think about how
you are all around me.
And that makes me feel happy.

Amen.
Grace

I want someone to play with

Dear Jesus,

I want someone to play with.
But everyone else already
has someone to play with.
Except me.
I feel sad and lonely.
Help me to remember just how
much you love me, Jesus.
Because that makes me feel better,
like I'm not all alone.
Because I know you are my friend.

Amen.